◆ Bath's unique mix of natural and man-made wonders have created one of the world's loveliest cities.

At its heart is the source of its name and fame - the mysterious hot mineral water springs. Over the centuries, these have attracted visitors who have come to wonder and worship, swallow or wallow in the water.

This pictorial guide spotlights Bath's carefully preserved historical, architectural, cultural and natural heritage. Complete with fold-out map, it is designed to help you enjoy the city to the full.
Highlights of Bath are numbered in the text so they can be easily located on the map inside the backcover.

◆ Die einzigartige Mischung aus den Naturwundern und den von Menschen geschaffenen Wunderwerken in Bath und seiner Umgebung haben sie zu einer der schönsten Städte der Welt werden lassen.

Den Kern der Stadt Bath bildet der Ursprung ihres Namens und ihrer Berühmtheit - die geheimnisvollen heißen Mineralquellen.

Dieser illustrierte Führer mit Stadtplan will Sie auf das sorgfältig erhaltene historische, architektonische, kulturelle und natürliche Erbe von Bath aufmerksam machen und soll Ihnen helfen, die Stadt in ihrer ganzen Fülle zu genießen
Die im Text angeg verweisen auf die im Stadtplan.

◆ Le mélange uni naturelles et créées par l'homme de Bath font de cette ville l'une des plus belles du monde.

C'est au coeur de cette cité que se trouve l'origine de son nom et de sa renommée - ses eaux de source chaudes mystérieuses.

Ce guide illustré met en valeur le patrimoine historique, architectural, culturel et naturel si bien préservés de Bath. Il contient un plan pour vous permettre de profiter au maximum de cette ville.
Les numéros indiqués dans le texte se trouvent sur le plan pour une identification facile.

Roman Baths Museum

◆ *The Roman Baths and Museum* (1). Water is the source of Bath's name and fame.

It gushes from a hot mineral spring at this spot at the rate of a quarter of a million gallons a day at a temperature of 117 degrees F, 46.5 degrees C.

Each droplet in the torrent started off as a raindrop that fell ten thousand years or more years ago on the nearby Mendip Hills. It has been on a fantastic journey, trickling through the rock, surging along huge underground gorges and rivers before being forced up from a depth of 2-3 miles from the earth's hot core to emerge at Bath.

Iron Age Celts hailed the spring sacred and worshipped their god Sul here.

The story of the healing powers of the water stretch back over 2,000 years to the legend of Prince Bladud, a leper who was banished from the court of his father King Lud. Working as a swineherd, he noticed that any pig with a skin disease who wallowed in the warm muddy spring waters was cured. He followed their example, became healed and was accepted back at his father's court. When he in turn became king, he is said to have shown his gratitude by building a bath around the healing spring.

After invading Britain in AD 43, the Romans investigated the steamy swampy spot in the Avon valley that was so revered by the local people.

In the space of 30-40 years, Roman efficiency and engineering ingenuity had drained the marsh, controlled and contained the water in a reservoir and built a temple and Britain's first health hydro.

They called their city Aquae Sulis (Sulis' Waters) and dedicated their temple to Sulis Minerva, their own goddess of healing.

A life-sized gilded bronze head of the goddess Minerva (photo below) is one of the prime exhibits in the museum. The stone head of Sul (the Gorgon's head) (photo page 3) which adorned the Roman temple is also on display.

The unfailing power of the hot spring (photo page 4) can be seen today as it tumbles from a reservoir through a Roman arch set on three mineral-stained stones.

Trinkhalle und Museum der Römischen Bäder

◆ *Die römischen Bäder und das Museum* (1). Wasser ist der Ursprung für den Namen der Stadt Bath und für ihre Berühmtheit.

Aus einer heißen Mineralquelle strömen an dieser Stelle täglich 1.136.000 Liter Wasser mit einer Temperatur von 46,5°C.

Jeder Tropfen dieses Stroms begann als ein Regentropfen, der vor zehntausend oder mehr Jahren auf die nahegelegenen Mendip Hills fiel.

Die Kelten der Eisenzeit verehrten die Quelle als heilig und machten sie zu einer Kultstätte für ihren Gott Sul.

Die Legenden über die Heilkräfte des Wassers reichen 2.000 Jahre zurück.

Nach ihrem Einfall in England im Jahr 43 AD untersuchten die Römer die von den Einheimischen so verehrte, dampfende, sumpfige Stelle im Avon-Tal.

Mit römischer Gründlichkeit und technischer Genialität hatten sie das Gebiet innerhalb von 30 bis 40 Jahren trockengelegt, die Quelle gefaßt und einen Tempel und die

Roman Baths Museum

◆ *Les "Roman Baths" et le "Museum"* (1). L'eau est à l'origine du nom et de la renommée de Bath.

Les eaux de source chaudes jaillissaient du sol ici avec un débit de plus d'un million de litres par jour, à une température de 46,5°C.

Chaque goutte de cette source provient à l'origine d'une goutte de pluie qui est tombée, il y a dix mille ans ou plus, sur les collines de Mendip à proximité.

Les Celtes de l'Age de Fer saluaient cette source sacrée et adoraient le Dieu Sul.

Des légendes concernant les pouvoirs curatifs des eaux remontent à plus de 2.000 ans.

Peu après l'invasion de la Grande-Bretagne par les Romains en 43 ap. J.-C., ils s'intéressèrent aux marécages de la vallée de l'Avon qui était un lieu vénéré par les habitants de la région.

En l'espace de 30-40 ans, grâce à leur ingéniosité technique et leur efficacité, ils parvinrent à assécher les marécages, retenir l'eau dans un réservoir et construire un temple et la première ville d'eau de Grande-Bretagne.

Ils appelèrent leur ville Aquae Sulis et dédièrent leur temple à Sulis Minerva, leur déesse de la guérison.

La tête en bronze doré, grandeur nature, de la déesse Minerva (photo page 2) est l'un des objets les plus importants de ce musée. La tête en pierre de Sul (Tête de Gorjon) (photo de gauche) qui orne le temple romain y est également exposée.

Le pouvoir infaillible de cette source chaude (photo page 4) est encore impressionnant aujourd'hui, lorsque l'eau jaillit avec force du réservoir avant de passer dans une série d'arches romaines sur trois pierres maculées par les minéraux au fil des siècles.

erste Kuranlage Großbritanniens gebaut.

Die Römer nannten ihre Stadt Aquae Sulis (Sulis Wasser) und weihten ihren Tempel der Sulis-Minerva, ihrer eigenen Göttin der Heilung.

Ein lebensgroßer vergoldeter Bronzekopf der Göttin Minerva (Foto Seite 2) ist eines der Prunkstücke des Museums. Der Steinkopf des Sul (Foto unten) (das Gorgonenhaupt), der den römischen Tempel schmückte, ist ebenfalls zu sehen.

Die unerschöpfliche Kraft der heißen Quelle (Foto Seite 4) ist am Überlauf des Reservoirs auch heute noch sichtbar, wo das Wasser durch einen römischen Bogen auf drei von Mineralien verfärbten Steine strömt.

◆ In front of the temple (which still lies buried) the sacrificial altar was set. Upon it were placed offerings to the gods and animal entrails were examined to foretell the future. Carved fragments of the altar form part of the museum's collection of artefacts from the Roman period.

Not all visitors to the baths were cured by the mineral waters. Monuments to the dead and stone coffins are also on display. Other important finds include wall panels depicting the Four Seasons, a pediment featuring the Goddess Luna and a fragment of a marine mosaic showing a dolphin and sea horses (photo page 2-3).

Development of the vast Roman complex was a continuous process stretching over four centuries. Its paying customers enjoyed heated rooms, saunas, a 'whirlpool', Turkish baths, exercise rooms, plunge pools and the most impressive feature of all, the Great Bath (photo pages 7&5). This spectacular 26 metres-long warm bathing pool, with its great barrel vaulted roof and windows, was the centrepiece of the baths complex. Hollow box tiles were cemented together for the roof, which discouraged the formation of cold droplets of condensation falling on the shoulders of the bathers below. Each box tile had the mark of the maker, and a sample of this engineering technology can be seen in a recess flanking the Great Bath.

Several tons of lead sheeting (which came from the flourishing mineworks in the Mendip Hills during the Roman period) lines the floor of the Great Bath. Alcoves

◆ Vor dem Tempel (der noch vergraben liegt) befand sich der Opferaltar, auf dem den Göttern Opfer dargebracht und Innereien von Tieren untersucht wurden, um aus ihnen die Zukunft vorherzusagen. Behauene Bruchstücke des Altars gehören zur Sammlung von Artefakten aus römischer Zeit, die im Museum ausgestellt sind.

Das Mineralwasser konnte aber nicht alle Besucher der Bäder heilen, und so umfaßt die Sammlung des Museums auch Grabmäler und Steinsärge. Weitere Funde sind Wandtafeln, die die vier Jahreszeiten darstellen, ein Giebeldreieck mit der Götting Luna und ein Bruchstück aus einem Mosaik, auf dem ein Delphin und Seepferdchen dragestellt sind (Foto Seite 2-3).

Der Bau des riesigen römischen Gebäudekomplexes erstreckte sich kontinuierlich über vier Jahrhunderte hinweg. Den zahlenden Kurgästen standen beheizte Räume, Saunen, ein

Model of the Roman Baths and Temple of Sulis Minerva as it would have appeared in the 4th century AD.

Die römischen Bäder und der Tempel der Sulis-Minerva, wie sie im vierten Jahrhundert AD aussahen.

Les "Roman Baths" et le temple de Sulis Minerva tels qu'ils se présentaient probablement au 4ème siècle ap. J.-C.

◆ Face au temple (toujours enseveli) se trouvait l'autel des sacrifices. On y plaçait des offrandes pour les dieux et des entrailles d'animaux étaient examinées pour prédire l'avenir. Des fragments sculptés de l'autel font partie de la collection d'objets oeuvrés de la période romaine.

Mais toutes les personnes qui venaient à Bath n'étaient pas forcément guéries. On y trouve en effet des monuments aux morts et des cercueils en pierre. D'autres découvertes importantes comprennent des panneaux muraux représentant les Quatre Saisons, un fronton dépeignant la déesse Luna et un fragment d'une mosaique marine représentant un dauphin et des hippocampes(photo page 2-3).

Le développement du vaste complexe romain fut un processus continu réalisé sur une période de

◆ along the sides of the Great Bath allowed onlookers to sit, gossip, read and relax, buy drink, food and souvenirs away from the splashes of the bathers. The pool is continually topped up by hot water running directly from the reservoir.

The Great Bath lay hidden for tens of centuries until it was discovered in the 1860s. Within the space of 20 years, the excited Victorians had acquired the surrounding property and pulled down overlying buildings so that the site could be excavated and the full size and splendour of the Great Bath could be seen by the public. The zealous Victorians did not simply stop at excavation, however. They added their own embellishments: all stone (including the statues) above shoulder level around the Great Bath dates from this time.

The excavations of the East Baths includes a semi circular bath set into a wall recess. Here, bathers immersed themselves to the neck. It is thought that attendants with bellows agitated the curative waters, making this a forerunner of today's jacuzzi. The East Baths display the foundations for the hypocaust rooms heated by hot air flowing under the floor. At the opposite end of the Great Bath can be seen the changing room (apodyterium), while in the hot rooms (caldarium) visitors enjoyed various treatments. Skin was scraped, oiled and cleaned, hair and hard skin removed. To close the pores, bathers moved through to the tepidarium to cool gently before an invigorating cold plunge in the Circular Bath (frigidarium) (photo page 8). An

◆ Kneippbecken, türkische Dampfbäder, Turnhallen, heiße Bäder, Behandlungsräume, kalte Bäder und vor allem das eindrucksvolle große Becken (Great Bath) (Foto Seite 7 und Seite 5) zur Verfügung. Dieses spektakuläre 26m lange Warmwasser-Schwimmbecken war Mittelstück der Bäderanlage. Ursprünglich befand es sich in einer großen Halle mit Fenstern und Tonnengewölbe. Das Dach wurde mit hohlen Backsteinen gebaut, die der Bildung von kalten Kondensationstropfen entgegenwirkten, damit diese nicht den Badenden auf die Schultern tropften.

Der Boden des großen Beckens ist mit Bleiplatten ausgelegt, die mehrere Tonnen wiegen.

◆ quatre siècles. Ses clients profitèrent des pièces chauffées, des saunas, du bain à remous, des bains turcs, des gymnases, des bains pour plonger et du "Great Bath" (ou Grand Bain) (photo page 7 et page 5), le plus impressionnant de tous. Cette piscine spectaculaire de 26 mètres de long était l'élément central du complexe thermal. Il s'agissait à l'origine d'une grande salle avec fenêtres et toiture voûtée. Des tuiles creuses furent cimentées pour former la toiture afin d'empêcher les gouttelettes de condensation de tomber sur les épaules des baigneurs qui se trouvaient en dessous.

Plusieurs tonnes de feuilles de plomb tapissent le fond du "Great Bath". Des alcôves le long du "Great Bath" permettaient aux personnes

Das große Becken lag viele Jahrhunderte lang verborgen und wurde erst in den sechziger Jahren des 19. Jahrhunderts entdeckt. Der Eifer seiner viktorianischen Entdecker endete aber nicht bei der Ausgrabung. Sie fügten ihre eigenen Verzierungen hinzu: Alle Steinarbeiten (einschließlich der Statuen) über Schulterhöhe um das große Becken herum stammen aus dieser Zeit.

Die Ausgrabungen des Ostbäderteils (East Baths) des Gebäudekomplexes brachten ein in einer Nische angeordnetes halbkreisförmiges Kneippbecken zutage, in denen die Kurgäste sich Tauchbädern unterzogen. In den Ostbädern sind die Fundamente der Hypocaust-Räume zu sehen, die

qui ne se baignaient pas de s'asseoir, bavarder, lire ou se détendre.

Le "Great Bath" est resté enseveli pendant des dizaines de siècles jusqu'à sa découverte en 1860. Les Victoriens enthousiastes ne se sont cependant pas contentés de faire des excavations. Ils ont ajouté leurs propres ornements: toutes les pierres situées à hauteur d'épaule et plus haut autour du "Great Bath" datent de cette époque.

Les excavations de la partie est du complexe thermal inclut un bassin semi-circulaire dans un renfoncement dans le mur où les baigneurs s'y plongaient jusqu'au cou. Les Thermes Est exposent les fondations des hypocaustes chauffés par de l'air chaud passant dans le plancher. A l'autre extrémité du "Great Bath" on peut voir les

◆ intensely hot area was called a laconicum.

The Roman central heating system was sophisticated and efficient. Hot air heated by a furnace outside the rooms was drawn by ducted flue through the rooms and under the flooring which was raised on piles. Hollow box tiles were used to build hot 'igloos' and to ensure even underfloor heat (photo page 6).

Roman arched windows overlook the King's Bath (photo page 6). Through here, visitors threw offerings into the water to the gods as this is the site of the sacred

◆ mit unter dem Fußboden strömender Heißluft geheizt wurden. Am gegenüberliegenden Ende des großen Beckens befindet sich der Umkleideraum (Apodyterium), während die warmen Räume (Caldarium) für verschiedenen Behandlungen benutzt wurden. Hier wurde die Haut geschabt, geölt und gereinigt, Haar und Hornhaut entfernt. Zum Schließen der Poren begaben sich die Badegäste dann zum Tepidarium, wo sie sich vor dem belebenden Sprung ins kalte runde Bad (Frigidarium) (Foto Seite 8) sanft abkühlten.

◆ vestiaires (apodyterum), et dans les salles chaudes (caldarium), les baigneurs recevaient divers traitements. On leur frottait, huilait et nettoyait la peau, et on les épilait et éliminait les callosités. Pour resserrer les pores de la peau, les baigneurs passaient dans le tepidarium pour se rafraîchir en douceur avant de faire un plongeon revigorant dans le bain circulaire (frigidarium) (photo page 8).

Le système de chauffage central romain était sophistiqué et efficace. L'air chaud, chauffé par un four en dehors des salles, était aspiré dans des conduites à travers les pièces et

◆ spring and reservoir. Offerings for good luck included carved gemstones, earrings and coins (photo above). They also threw in a selection of lead curses calling for divine retribution against those who had tricked or displeased them. Votive offerings – including cups, and an oil lamp – have also been found.

Statues placed in the water by the Romans gave a spectacular, theatrical vision shimmering through the rising steam of people walking on water.

There is evidence that customers travelled from far and wide throughout the Roman Empire to visit the vast baths development that flourished nearly two thousand years ago.

When the Romans left Britain in AD 410, the natives lacked the necessary expertise to cope with the problems of silting and flooding. The site rapidly returned to its original state - a marsh. Masonry sunk and collapsed into it. Yet the principal hot spring still gushed and monks ran a healing centre around what remained. Even through its obscure days, visitors still came to drink and bathe. Records show that five medieval baths were in use in the 16th century, but they had a sleazy and squalid reputation.

A visit in the early 1600s from Anne, wife of King James I, to seek a cure for dropsy signalled the start of Bath's revival. Anne was followed by a selection of visiting royals. These led to Bath's reconstruction during the 18th century.

◆ Die römische Zentralheizung war ein hochentwickeltes und wirksames System. Von einem Ofen außerhalb der Räume erwärmte Heißluft wurde von Heizluftkanälen durch die Räume und unter dem auf Pfählen getragenen Fußboden hindurch geführt (Foto Seite 6).

Durch die römischen Bogenfenster, die das Königsbad (King's Bath) (Foto Seite 6) überblicken, warfen Besucher Opfergaben für die Götter in das Wasser, da sich an dieser Stelle die heilige Quelle und das Reservoir befanden. Zu den als Glücksbringer hier hineingeworfenen Gegenständen gehören Silber-, Bronze- und Zinnbecher, -teller, -gefäße und eine Öllampe, Gemmen, Ohrringe und Münzen (Foto oben).

Es gibt Beweise dafür, daß Kurgäste aus dem ganzen römischen Reich anreisten, um die riesige Bäderanlage zu besuchen, die hier vor fast zweitausend Jahren ihre Blütezeit hatte.

◆ sous le plancher qui était surélevé et reposait sur des pilots (photo 6).

Les fenêtres romaines à arches donnaient sur le "King's Bath" (photo page 6). C'est par ces fenêtres que les visiteurs jetaient leurs offrandes aux Dieux dans l'eau, car c'est l'emplacement du réservoir et de la source sacrés. Les offrandes pour s'assurer une bonne fortune comprenaient timbales, assiettes et plats en argent, bronze et étain et une lampe à huile; des pierres précieuses taillées, boucles d'oreille et pièces (photo ci-dessus).

On a des preuves que les clients venaient des quatre coins de l'empire romain pour visiter le vaste aménagement thermal prospère il y a près de deux mille ans.

Lorsque les Romains quittèrent la Grande-Bretagne en l'an 410 ap.

Als die Römer 410 AD aus Großbritannien abzogen, fehlte es den Einheimischen an der erforderlichen Fachkenntnis, um mit den Verschlammungs- und Überschwemmungsproblemen fertig zu werden. Die Anlage wurde in kurzer Zeit wieder zu dem, was sie ursprünglich war - nämlich einem Sumpf. Die Hauptquelle sprudelte jedoch immer noch. Um die Reste der Bäderanlage unterhielten Mönche ein Heilzentrum. Auch während der Zeit, in der sie wieder mehr oder weniger in Vergessenheit geraten war, kamen noch Besucher, um das Wasser zu trinken und darin zu baden.

Ein Besuch durch Anne, Gemahlin von König James I, die ein Heilmittel für Wassersucht suchte, kündigte den Beginn der zweiten Blütezeit von Bath an. Nach Anne besuchten noch andere Mitglieder der königlichen Familie die Stadt, was zur Sanierung von Bath im 18. Jahrhundert führte.

J.C., les natifs ne possédaient pas les compétences nécessaires pour faire face aux problèmes d'envasement et d'inondations. Le site retourna rapidement à son état d'origine - un marécage. Mais la source chaude principale coulait toujours et des moines établirent un centre de guérisons autour de ce qu'il en restait. Même durant les périodes où Bath était moins connue, les visiteurs y venaient toujours pour boire son eau et s'y baigner.

Une visite de la reine Anne, épouse du roi Jacques Ier, au début du 17ème siècle, pour essayer de guérir son hydropisie, marqua le début du renouveau de Bath. La reine Anne fut suivie par plusieurs membres illustres de la famille royale. Ceci a conduit à la reconstruction de Bath au 18ème siècle.

Pump Room

◆ The city's Georgian heyday is celebrated in the *Pump Room* (2) (photo below), built above the baths complex.

To this elegant room, designed by Thomas Baldwin, fashionable society made their regular visits to drink the waters. Three glasses in the morning were recommended by physicians. The water, a cocktail of 40 different minerals and elements, is still dispensed from an elegant fountain, called the King's Spring, (photo right) although doctors today are sceptical of its powers to ease skin diseases or rheumatic and arthritic conditions.

Overseeing the Pump Room is a statue of Richard 'Beau' Nash, a gambler who became the uncrowned king of Bath. His title was Master of Ceremonies and he set the social, dress and etiquette standards for the city in the Georgian period. His role was to preside over banquets, breakfasts, dances and musical entertainments.

Both inside and out, the Pump Room is decorated with classical columns. A Greek inscription above the entrance bears the legend: Water is Best.

Trinkhalle

◆ Die georgianische Glanzzeit der Stadt spiegelt sich in *der Trinkhalle* (2) (Foto unten) über dem Bäderkomplex wieder.

In diesen von Thomas Baldwin entworfenen eleganten Raum kamen die Vornehmen der britischen Gesellschaft regelmäßig zur Trinkkur. Das Wasser enthält 40 Minerale und Spurenelemente und wird auch heute noch an einem eleganten Brunnen, Königsquelle (King's Spring) genannt, ausgegeben (Foto rechts).

In der Trinkhalle steht eine Statue von Richard "Beau" Nash, einem Glücksspieler, der zum ungekrönten König der Stadt wurde. Sein Titel war "Zeremonienmeister". Er gab in der georgianischen Epoche den gesellschaftlichen Ton an und setzte die Maßstäbe für Kleidung und Etikette für die Stadt. Seine Aufgabe war es, über Bankette, Frühstücke, Bälle und musikalische Unterhaltungsveranstaltungen zu präsidieren.

Der Trinksaal ist außen und innen mit klassischen Säulen verziert. Die griechische Inschrift über dem Eingang besagt: Wasser ist am besten.

Pump Room

◆ L'apogée de la ville Georgienne est célébrée dans *la "Pump Room"* (2) (photo de gauche) située au-dessus du complexe thermal.

C'est dans cette salle magnifique, dessinée par Thomas Baldwin, que le beau monde venait régulièrement boire les eaux. On peut toujours y boire l'eau, composée de 40 minéraux et éléments différents, qui jaillit d'une belle fontaine appelée "King's Spring" (Source du roi).

La "Pump Room" est dominée par la statue de Richard "Beau" Nash, un joueur qui devint le roi sans couronne de Bath. On l'appelait "Maître des Cérémonies" et il établit les normes en termes de vie sociale, de mode et d'étiquette pour la ville Georgienne. Son rôle consistait à présider les banquets, les petits déjeuners, les soirées dansantes et les divertissements musicaux.

La "Pump Room" est ornée, à l'intérieur et à l'extérieur, de colonnes classiques. On peut lire l'inscription en Grec suivante au-dessus de l'entrée: "L'eau est ce qu'il y a de meilleur".

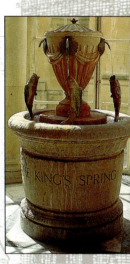

Bath Abbey

◆ Through the peaks and troughs of Bath's history, *the Abbey* (3) has stood dominant for five centuries at its centre.

The site has been in continuous use for Christian worship since 676. Edgar, the first King of all England, was crowned in the Saxon Abbey in 973 and all coronations since then have been based on that original ceremony.

In 1088, John de Villula was appointed Bishop of Bath and created a new cathedral so immense that the present Abbey stands within its nave. A fire in 1137 damaged the structure which was then left to decay, although visitors can glimpse the stone bases of the old cathedral, built nearly a thousand years ago.

A bishop's dream led to the building of the Abbey as its stands today. Bishop Oliver King, former chief secretary to King Henry VII, had a dream in which he saw angels going up and down ladders reaching to heaven. He heard voices saying "Let an olive establish the crown and a king restore the church." Bishop King interpreted this as a sign he should rebuild the Abbey. Work started in 1499.

Two master masons, Robert and William Vertue, promised him the "finest vault in England" and the Abbey's fan vaulting is its most impressive feature. The brothers built King Henry VII's chapel at Westminster and William, after Robert's death, built St George's Chapel at Windsor Castle.

Bath Abbey

◆ *Die Abtei* (3) steht schon seit fünf Jahrhunderten beherrschend im Mittelpunkt der Stadt, deren gute und schlechte Zeiten sie miterlebt hat.

Das Gelände der Abtei in Bath dient schon seit 676 ohne Unterbrechung als christliche Andachtsstätte. Edgar, der erste König von England, wurde 973 in der angelsächsischen Abtei gekrönt.

1088 wurde John de Villula zum Bischof von Bath ernannt. Er ließ eine neue Kathedrale bauen, deren Ausmaße so riesig waren, daß die heutige Abtei in ihrem Hauptschiff steht. 1137 beschädigte ein Feuer das Gebäude, das dann dem Verfall preisgegeben wurde. Besucher können jedoch noch die vor fast tausend Jahren gebauten Steinfundamente der alten Kathedrale ausmachen.

Der Traum eines Bischofs führte zum Bau des Abteigebäudes, wie wir es heute kennen. Bischof Oliver King, der ehemalige Hauptsekretär von Heinrich VII, hatte einen Traum, in dem er Engel auf Leitern in den Himmel hinauf- und von dort heruntersteigen sah. Er hörte Stimmen, die sagen "Let an olive establish the crown and a king restore the church" (bedeutet ungefähr: "Laßt eine Olive die Krone einführen und einen König die Kirche wiederherstellen"). Bischof King deutete dieses als ein Zeichen, daß er die Abtei wieder aufbauen sollte. Mit der Arbeit wurde 1499 begonnen.

L'Abbaye de Bath

◆ Tout au long de l'histoire de Bath qui a connu des hauts et des bas selon les époques, *l'Abbaye* (3) en a dominé le centre pendant cinq siècles.

Ce site religieux a été utilisé continuellement pour le culte chrétien depuis l'an 676. Edgar, le premier roi de toute l'Angleterre fut couronnée dans l'Abbaye saxonne en 973.

En 1088, Jean de Villula fut nommé Evêque de Bath et créa une cathédrale d'une telle envergure que l'abbaye actuelle tient dans sa nef. En 1137, un incendie endommagea la structure qui se détériora par la suite, mais les visiteurs peuvent toujours apercevoir les bases en pierre de l'ancienne cathédrale, construite il y a près de mille ans.

Le rêve d'un évêque est à l'origine de la construction de l'Abbaye telle qu'on la connaît aujourd'hui. L'Evêque Oliver King, ancien secrétaire principal du roi Henri VII, fit en effet un rêve dans lequel il vit des anges montant et descendant des échelles conduisant au paradis. Il entendit des voix disant "Let an olive establish the crown and a king restore the church" (Une olive établira la couronne et un roi restaurera l'église). L'évêque King interpréta ceci comme étant un signe pour la reconstruction de l'Abbaye. Les travaux commencèrent ainsi en 1499.

Deux maîtres maçons, Robert et William Vertue, lui promirent la "plus belle voûte d'Angleterre" et les voûtes constituent maintenant la particularité la plus impressionnante de cette Abbaye.

Les travaux de construction furent arrêtés par la Dissolution des Monastères décrétée par le roi Henri VIII en 1539 et reprirent en 1574

◆ Building work was stopped by King Henry VIII's Dissolution of the Monasteries in 1539. Work restarted in 1574 when Queen Elizabeth I visited Bath. Her godson Sir John Harington took her to the church during a thunderstorm and she was so shocked by the incomplete Abbey she ordered collections to be made throughout England for seven years to fund repairs.

Bishop Montagu took up the restoration challenge with an enthusiastic renovation programme during his eight years as bishop between 1608-1616. Bishop Montagu's brother Sir Henry donated the carved oak west doors in 1617.

While the structure was little altered, hundreds of memorial plaques were added to the walls in the 18th and 19th centuries, including one to Richard 'Beau' Nash. The Abbey bells then rang for important visitors - or for anyone else who could afford the half a crown fee.

The Victorians added pinnacles, flying buttresses and the stone fan vaulting in the nave (photos pages 11-12) which mason Vertue originally planned 350 years earlier.

In 1923, the Choir Vestry was added in memory of those who died in the 1914-19 war.

The Abbey is regarded as an outstanding example of Perpendicular Gothic architecture, and is one of the last great churches built in this style.

Viewed from Abbey Churchyard (photo page 10), its west front symbolically depicts Bishop Oliver King's dream of ladders reaching to heaven with falling and rising angels (photo right). Saints Peter and Paul, to whom the church is dedicated, stand on either side of the carved oak door. Over the door is a statue of King Henry VII. A bishop's mitre surmounts an olive tree growing through a king's crown, to form a rebus or signature in stone.

The Abbey is called the "lantern of the west" as it features more window than wall.

On the south side of the Abbey you can find the Heritage Vaults.

The recently restored eighteenth century cellars now house a fascinating exhibition which takes the visitor through 1600 years of Christian history at the Abbey in sights and sounds (photo top right).

◆ Zwei Meistersteinmetzen, Robert und William Vertue, versprachen ihm das "feinste Gewölbe in England". Die Fächergewölbedecke der Abtei ist auch wirklich das beeindruckendste Merkmal des Gebäudes.

Die Bauarbeiten wurden durch die von Heinrich VIII erlassene Auflösung der Kloster 1539 unterbrochen. Sie wurden nach einem Besuch von Königin Elisabeth I in Bath 1574 wieder aufgenommen. Während eines Gewitters brachte ihr Patensohn Sir John Harington sie in die Kirche, und Elisabeth I war so schockiert über die unvollständige Abtei, daß sie anordnete, daß in ganz England sieben Jahre lang Kollekten zur Finanzierung der Reparaturen erhoben werden sollten.

Bischof Montagu nahm während seiner achtjährigen Amtszeit von 1608 bis 1616 die Herausforderung der Restaurierung mit einem enthusiastischen Renovierungsprogramm an. Sein Bruder Sir Henry stiftete 1617 die geschnitzten eichernen Westtüren.

Das Gebäude wurde im 18. und 19. Jahrhundert strukturell kaum geändert, an seinen Wänden wurden in dieser Zeit jedoch Hunderte von Gedenktafeln angebracht, darunter auch eine für Richard "Beau" Nash.

In viktorianischer Zeit erhielt die Abtei dann Fialen, Strebebögen und das steinerne Fächergewölbe im Hauptschiff (Fotos Seite 11-12), das Steinmetz Vertue schon 350 Jahre zuvor geplant hatte.

Die Abtei gilt als ein hervorragendes Beispiel der perpendikularen Gothik. Sie ist eine der letzten großen Kirchen, die in diesem Stil gebaut wurde.

An ihrer Westfront, vom Vorplatz der Kathedrale (Abbey Churchyard) (Foto Seite 10) gesehen, befindet sich die symbolische Darstellung von Bischof Oliver Kings Traum von in den Himmel reichenden Leitern mit fallenden und aufsteigenden Engeln (Foto rechts). Sankt Peter und Sankt Paul, denen die Kirche geweiht ist, stehen zu beiden Seiten der geschnitzten Eichentür. Über der Tür befindet sich eine Statue von Heinrich VII. Eine Bischofsmütze krönt einen Olivenbaum, der durch eine Königskrone wächst, und bildet ein Rebus (Bilderrätsel) oder eine Signatur in Stein.

Die Abtei wird die "Laterne des Westens" genannt, da sie mehr Fenster- als Wandfläche aufweist.

Auf der Südseite der Abtei befindet sich das Abteimuseum, "Heritage Vaults" gennant.

Im kürzlich renovierten Kellergewölbe aus dem 18. Jahrhundert befindet sich jetzt eine faszinierende Ausstellung, die den Besucher optisch und akustisch durch 1600 Jahre christlicher Geschichte in der Abtei führt.

◆ lorsque la reine Elisabeth Ire visita Bath. Son filleul, Sir John Harington, l'emmena dans cette église pendant un orage et elle fut tellement choquée par cette Abbaye inachevée qu'elle donna l'ordre de faire des quêtes dans toute l'Angleterre pendant sept ans afin de pouvoir faire les réparations nécessaires.

L'Évêque Montagu releva le défi de la restauration grâce à un programme de rénovation dynamique au cours de ses huit ans en sa qualité d'évêque de 1608-1616. Son frère, Sir Henry, fit don des portes ouest, en chêne sculpté, en 1617.

Bien que l'on ait apporté peu de changements à la structure de l'Abbaye, des centaines de plaques commémoratives en ont progressivement couvert les murs au cours des 18ème et 19ème siècles, dont une en l'honneur de Richard "Beau" Nash.

A l'époque victorienne on y ajouta des pinacles, des arcs-boutants et les voûtes en éventail, en pierre (photos pages 11-12) dans la nef que le maçon Vertue avait prévu 350 ans auparavant.

L'Abbaye est un exemple remarquable du style d'architecture Gothique Perpendiculaire, et est l'une des dernières églises extraordinaires construites dans ce style.

Depuis l'Abbey Churchyard (photo page 10), on peut voir sa façade ouest qui dépeint symboliquement le rêve de l'Évêque Oliver King avec ses échelles montant vers le paradis et ses anges les montant et descendant (photo de droite). Saint-Pierre et Saint-Paul à qui cette église est dédiée, encadrent la porte en chêne sculpté et au-dessus de cette porte se trouve une statue du roi Henri VIII. Une mitre d'évêque surmonte un olivier qui pousse à travers une couronne de roi, pour former un rébus ou une signature de pierre.

On appelle l'Abbaye la "lanterne de l'ouest", car elle possède plus de vitraux que de murs.

A l'extrémité sud de l'Abbaye, on peut découvrir les "Heritage Vaults".

Ces caves du 18ème siècle, récemment restaurées, accueillent maintenant une exposition fascinante qui raconte aux touristes 1600 ans d'histoire chrétienne dans cette Abbaye au moyen d'une bande sonore qui vient renforcer le plaisir des yeux.

Bath's Georgian Gems

◆ The glorious years of 18th century Georgian Bath are reflected today in its golden stone buildings.

Three men transformed the city - Richard 'Beau' Nash, a gambler; Ralph Allen, an entrepreneur and John Wood, an architect. The first provided the social tone, the second the stone and the third the classic style that set the standard for the city's development.

Abbey Churchyard (4), dominated by the Abbey's majestic west front, features a line of 18th century buildings which include the National Trust Shop. This was formerly the home of Major George Wade who financed Ralph Allen in his early business ventures in Bath.

Buskers (photo below) are now a regular feature in the Abbey Churchyard, although 300 years ago Daniel Defoe described the area as a centre for 'raffling, gaming and levity'.

Bath Street (5) has a graceful colonnade, built in 1789, to form a covered link between the main Pump Room and Baths to the Cross Bath which is fed by one of the city's three hot springs. In the 17th and 18th centuries, this bath was favoured by people of 'quality and rank'. A Roman reservoir lies beneath it.

The Royal Mineral Water Hospital (6) on the corner of Union Street and Upper Borough Walls was built by John Wood, using stone supplied by Ralph Allen financed by money collected from Bath's visitors by Richard 'Beau' Nash. The project was supported by Bath's leading physician, Dr William Oliver, who invented the Bath Oliver biscuit as an antidote to rich food. A guide to how patients fared after treatment at the hospital in the years 1742-1769 lists:
Cured 1,853; Much Better 2,773; Incurable 355; Improper 773; Irregular 78; Dead 169.

The hospital's £3 admission fee either paid the patient's fare home or for their burial.

Queen Street, with its cobbled roads and bow windows, is early Georgian. It is crossed by *Trim Street* (7) which features an arch across the road (photo right). General Wolfe, hero of the Battle of Quebec (1759) lived at number 5.

Bath - Seine Georgianischen Kostbarkeiten

◆ Die glorreichen Jahre des georgianischen Bath im 18. Jahrhundert werden heute noch in den goldfarbenen Steingebäuden reflektiert.

Die Verwandlung der Stadt wurde von drei Männern bewirkt - Richard "Beau" Nash, einem Glücksspieler, Ralph Allen, einem Unternehmer, und John Wood, einem Architekten. Der erste gab den gesellschaftlichen Ton an, der zweite lieferte das Baumaterial und der dritte den klassischen Stil, der die Maßstäbe für die sich entwickelnde Stadt Bath setzte.

Abbey Churchyard (4), der Vorplatz der Abtei, wird von der majestätischen Westfront der Abtei dominiert und ist durch eine Gebäudezeile aus dem 18. Jahrhundert gekennzeichnet. Eines dieser Gebäude war die Wohnung von Major George Wade, der Ralph Allen seine ersten Geschäftsunternehmungen in Bath finanzierte. Heute befindet sich hier ein National Trust Shop.

Straßenmusikanten (Foto links) gehören heute zum regelmäßigen Erscheinungsbild des Abbey Churchyard.

Bath Street (5) hat eine elegante Kolonnade, die im Jahr 1789 erbaut wurde und eine überdachte Verbindung zwischen der Trinkhalle (Pump Room) mit den Bädern und dem Kreuzbad (Cross Bath) bildet, das aus einer der drei heißen Quellen der Stadt gespeist wird. Im 17. und 18. Jahrhundert wurde dieses Bad von Menschen von "Qualität und Rang" bevorzugt. Unter dem Kreuzbad liegt ein römisches Reservoir.

Das Royal Mineral Water Hospital (6), das Mineralwasserkrankenhaus, an der Ecke von Union Street und Upper Borough Walls wurde von John Wood mit Stein aus Ralph Allens Steinbruch gebaut. Finanziert wurde der Bau mit Spenden, die Richard "Beau" Nash von Besuchern der Stadt erbat. Das Projekt wurde vom führenden Arzt der Stadt, Dr. William Oliver, unterstützt. Dr. Oliver erfand das Bath Oliver Biscuit, ein Gebäck, als verdauungsförderndes Gegenmittel zu schweren Speisen.

Queen Street mit ihrem Straßenpflaster und ihren Runderkern ist frühgeorgianisch. Sie wird von der von einem Bogen überspannten *Trim Street* (7) (Foto oben) überkreuzt.

Les Merveilles de la ville Georgienne de Bath

◆ Les années glorieuses de la ville Georgienne de Bath au 18ème siècle se reflètent aujourd'hui dans ses bâtiments en pierre dorée.

Trois hommes transformèrent la ville - Richard "Beau" Nash, joueur invétéré, Ralph Allen, homme d'affaires et John Wood, architecte. Le premier organisa la vie sociale de Bath, le second fournit la pierre célèbre et le troisième, le style classique qui fut choisi pour toute la ville.

L'Abbey Churchyard (4), dominé par la façade ouest majestueuse, présente une série de bâtiments alignés datant du 18ème siècle dont le magasin du National Trust. Ceci était jadis la demeure du Major George Wade, qui finança Ralph Allen au début de ses activités commerciales à Bath.

On voit souvent des artistes jouer dans l'Abbey Churchyard (photo page 14).

Bath Street (5), possède d'élégantes colonnades bâties en 1789 pour former un passage couvert entre la "Pump Room" et les est alimenté par l'une des trois sources chaudes de la ville. Aux 17ème et 18ème siècles, ce bain était le bain de prédilection des gens de "qualité et de haut rang". Un réservoir romain se trouve sous ce bain.

Le Royal Mineral Water Hospital (6), à l'angle d'Union Street et de "Upper Borough Walls" a été construit par John Wood, à l'aide des pierres fournies par Ralph Allen financées avec l'argent recueilli auprès des visiteurs par Richard "Beau" Nash. Ce projet reçut le soutien de l'illustre médecin de Bath, Dr. William Oliver, qui inventa les biscuits "Bath Oliver" comme antidote contre la nourriture riche.

Queen Street, avec ses routes pavées et ses fenêtres en saillie, date du début de la période Georgienne. *Trim Street* (7) qui la traverse est caractérisée par une arche au-dessus de la route (photo ci-dessus).

◆ *Queen Square* (8) was the first major project of architect John Wood two years after he arrived in Bath from London with a flair for what was fashionable. Queen Square (photo below), begun in 1729, was named after Caroline, wife of King George II. The square was Wood's interpretation of the Palladian architectural style. Planned to resemble a palace with forecourt, the north side has a grand facade with bays and Corinthian columns. John Wood himself lived in the square he designed. Dr William Oliver was another famous resident. Number 13 is just one of the houses occupied by authoress Jane Austen when she visited the city. The central obelisk commemorates the visit of Frederick, Prince of Wales.

Royal Crescent (9) is one of Bath's spectacular sights (photo page 18-19). Built in a 200 metre sweeping arc, its 30 houses stand behind a flourish of 114 Ionic columns. The Crescent, described as the finest in Europe, represents the peak of Palladian style architecture in the city. Its hilltop position gives unrivalled views over Bath.

Number 1 Royal Crescent (10) is now a museum which recreates an authentic Georgian interior (photo page 20) in one of the Bath's most fashionable addresses. It is restored to the style enjoyed by its former

◆ *Queen Square* (8) (Foto unten) war das erste größere Projekt des Architekten John Wood. Die Bauarbeiten begannen 1729, und benannt wurde der Platz nach Caroline, der Gemahlin von König George II. Der Platz war Woods Interpretation des Palladium-Architekturstils. John Wood wohnte selbst in einem der Gebäude dieses von ihm entworfenen Platzes. Ein weiterer berühmter Anlieger war Dr. William Oliver. Die berühmte Schriftstellerin Jane Austen wohnte während ihrer Besuche in Bath unter anderem auch in Haus Nr. 13.

Royal Crescent (9) ist eine der spektakulärsten Sehenswürdigkeiten von Bath (Foto Seite 18-19). Es wird als das beste halbmondförmige Gebäude in Europa beschrieben und repräsentiert den Höhepunkt der Palladium-Architektur in der Stadt. Seine 30 Häuser stehen hinter einer Fassade mit 114 ionischen Säulen auf einem 200 m langen weitläufigen Bogen.

Royal Crescent Number 1 (10) (Foto Seite 20) ist heute ein Museum, in dem die authentische georgianische Innenausstattung an einer der begehrtesten Anschriften in Bath wiederhergestellt wurde. Das Haus wurde in dem von seinen früheren illustren Bewohnern, zu denen im Jahr 1796 der Herzog von York und

◆ *Queen Square* (8) (photo ci-dessous) a été le premier grand projet de l'architecte John Wood. Queen Square, commencé en 1729, dat son nom à la reine Caroline, épouse du roi George II. Cette place était l'interprétation du style palladien de Wood. John Wood a lui-même a habité sur cette place. Dr. William Oliver en fut aussi un résident célèbre. Le numéro 13 est l'une seulement des maisons occupées par l'écrivain Jane Austen lorsqu'elle visitait la ville.

Royal Crescent (9) est l'un des sites les plus spectaculaires de Bath (photo pages 18-19). Construites en une majestueuse courbe continue de 200 mètres, ses 30 maisons sont parées de 114 colonnes ioniques. Cette rue en arc de cercle, décrite comme la plus belle d'Europe, représente l'apogée du style palladien dans la ville.

Le no.1 de "*Royal Crescent*" (10), l'une des adresses actuellement les plus cotées de Bath, est aujourd'hui un musée recréant un intérieur authentique Georgien (photo page 20). Il est restauré dans le style tant apprécié par ses occupants illustres, dont le Duc de York en 1796 et la Princesse de Lamballe,

◆ illustrious residents, who included the Duke of York in 1796 and the Princess de Lamballe, Lady-in-Waiting to Marie Antoinette of France.

Sir Isaac Pitman, inventor of the Pitman system of shorthand, lived at number 17. Elizabeth Linley eloped from number 11 with statesman and dramatist Sheridan.

Royal Cresent is linked (via Brock Street) to another of Bath's stately and outstanding Georgian features: *the Circus* (11) (photo page 22-23). They represent the work of a famous father and son: John Wood the Elder designed the Circus and his son John complemented his design with the Crescent. John Wood the Elder was fired and inspired to recreate the great imperial structures of Rome itself in Bath and the Circus is considered his greatest design. He did not live to see his design translated into stone. After he died in 1754, his son saw the project to completion. It consists of three curved crescents which form a circle some 100 metres in diameter. The terraces all display a unified front featuring the three classical design forms, Doric, Ionic and Corinthian, and a frieze showing symbols of the arts and occupations.

Famous residents included Dr David Livingstone, the missionary and explorer; Lord Clive of India; Thomas Gainsborough the painter and William Pitt, MP and Prime Minister.

◆ Prinzessin de Lamballe, Hofdame der Marie Antoinette von Frankreich zählten, genossenen Stil renoviert.

Royal Crescent ist über die Brock Street mit einem weiteren der imposanten und außergewöhnlichen georgianischen Wahrzeichen von Bath - *dem Circus* (11) - verbunden (Foto Seite 22-23). Die beiden sind das Werk eines berühmten Vaters und seines Sohnes: John Wood sen. entwarf den Circus und sein Sohn John ergänzte seinen Entwurf mit dem Royal Crescent. Der Circus, der in Bath selbst an die großartigen Bauten Roms erinnern soll, wird als der beste Entwurf von John Wood sen. bezeichnet. Er verstarb jedoch, bevor sein Entwurf realisiert wurde. Nach seinem Tod im Jahr 1754 führte sein Sohn das Projekt aus. Drei halbmondförmige Gebäude bilden einen Kreis mit einem Durchmesser von etwa 100 m. An den einheitlich gestalteten Fronten der Reihenhäuser finden sich die drei klassischen Architekturformen - dorische, ionische und korinthische Säulen - und ein Fries mit Symbolen der Künste und Berufe.

◆ dame d'honneur de Marie-Antoinette.

"Royal Crescent" est relié (via Brock Street) à un autre chef-d'oeuvre Georgien remarquable et majestueux: *le "Circus"* (11) (photo pages 22-23). C'est l'oeuvre d'un père et d'un fils célèbres: John Wood Père a conçu le "Circus" et son fils vint compléter cette création avec le "Crescent". John Wood Père voulait recréer les grandes structures impériales de Rome à Bath et le "Circus" est considéré comme sa plus belle oeuvre. Il mourut malheureusement avant que son dessin ne soit concrétisé en pierre. Après sa mort, en 1754, son fils termina ce projet. Il est composé de trois rues formant un cercle de 100 mètres de diamètre. Les terrasses présentent toutes un front homogène avec trois styles classiques, dorique, ionique et corinthien, et une frise dépeignant des symboles d'arts et de professions.

◆ *The Assembly Rooms* (12) in Bennett Street were the social centre of late Georgian Bath. The fashionable flocked there to dine and dance, gossip and gamble, to flirt and flaunt their finery and to see and be seen. The social pecking order was rigorously observed within its elegant suite of rooms. The Assembly Rooms were designed and built by John Wood the Younger and built between 1769-71. Known as the Upper Rooms, they were in continual use from serving 2,000 people for public breakfasts to grand balls. Johann Strauss, Liszt, Rubenstein and Charles Dickens were among the many who performed there.

Now restored after war damage and a lapse into decay and indignity as a cinema and saleroom, the Assembly Rooms include a ballroom which is the largest 18th century room in Bath. Its chandeliers were made by William Parker of Fleet Street, London. Other rooms include the Octagon Card Room, the Long Card Room and Tea Room

◆ *Die Assembly Rooms* (Versammlungsräume) (12) in der Bennett Street bildeten den gesellschaftlichen Mittelpunkt des spätgeorgianischen Bath. Hier trafen sich die Vornehmen in Scharen zu Essen und Tanz, zu Klatsch und Glücksspiel, zum Flirten und Prahlen und um zu sehen und gesehen zu werden. In diesen eleganten Räumen wurde die gesellschaftliche Rangordnung strengstens eingehalten. Die Assembly Rooms wurden von John Wood jun. entworfen und zwischen 1769 und 1771 gebaut, waren sie unter der Bezeichnung "Upper Rooms" ständig in Gebrauch, angefangen vom Frühstück für 2.000 Personen bis hin zu großen Gesellschaftsbällen. Johann Strauß, Liszt, Rubenstein und Charles Dickens und viele andere traten hier auf.

Die Räume waren im Krieg beschädigt worden und dann als Kino und Verkaufsraum Zerfall ausgesetzt, ihre frühere Pracht wurde aber schließlich

◆ *Les Assembly Rooms* (12) dans Bennett Street étaient le centre social de la ville Georgienne de Bath. Les gens du beau monde y dînaient, dansaient, bavardaient, jouaient, flirtaient et faisaient parade de leurs richesses; ils voulaient s'y rencontrer et être vus. La hiérarchie sociale était rigoureusement observée dans sa suite de pièces magnifiques. Les "Assembly Rooms" ont été conçues par John Wood Fils et construites entre 1769 et 1771. Appelées les "Upper Rooms", elles furent très fréquentées, servant jusqu'à 2000

◆ (photo page 23). Surrounding the suite of rooms are corridors known as 'corridors of scandal' where ladies retired from the exertions of the social whirl to cool off by exchanging hot gossip.

Doris Langley Moore's world famous Museum of Costume is housed in the Assembly Rooms and features fashions from the late 16th century to the present (Photo below).

While fashionable society of quality and status danced and dined at the Assembly Rooms, wealthy traders of Bath who were kept out sought a rival venue for their own gatherings: the *Banqueting Room* (13) in the Guildhall (Photo page 25). This exquisite room in the Adam style is hung with portraits by Reynolds and three Whitefriars glass chandeliers. It was opened in 1776, originally designed by Thomas Baldwin for use as the Town Hall.

◆ wiederhergestellt. Zu den Assembly Rooms gehört ein Ballsaal, der der größte Raum aus dem 18. Jahrhundert in Bath ist, der Octagon Card Room (achteckiges Kartenzimmer), der Long Card Room (langes Kartenzimmer) und der Tea Room (Teesaal) (Foto Seite 23). Die Räume sind von "Korridore der Skandale" genannten Korridoren umgeben, in die sich die Damen von den Anstrengungen der gesellschaftlichen Hektik zurückzogen, um sich beim Austausch des neuesten Klatsches abzukühlen.

Doris Langley Moores weltberühmtes Trachtenmuseum befindet sich ebenfalls in den Assembly Rooms. Es enthält Moden vom späten 16. Jahrhundert bis zur Gegenwart (Foto unten).

Die modebewußten Vornehmen der Gesellschaft veranstalteten ihre Bankette und Bälle in den Assembly Rooms, aber reiche Kaufleute von Bath, die dazu nicht eingeladen wurden, suchten sich einen Austragungsort für ihre eigenen Veranstaltungen - den Bankettsaal, *Banqueting Room* (13) genannt, im Rathaus (Guildhall). Dieser prächtige Saal (Foto Seite 25) wurde vom Architekten Adam entworfen und 1776 eröffnet. Hier hängen Porträts von Reynolds und drei Whitefriars-Glaskronleuchter.

◆ personnes pour les petits déjeuners et les grands bals. Johann Strauss, Listz, Rubenstein et Charles Dickens jouèrent ici.

Maintenant restaurées après les dommages de la guerre, leur détérioration et leur usage indigne en guise de salle de cinéma et salle des ventes, ces pièces comprennent la plus grande salle de bal de Bath au 18ème siècle et d'autres pièces telles que la salle "Octagon Card Room", la "Long Card Room" et la "Tea Room" (photo page 23). Elles étaient entourées de couloirs connus sous le nom de "couloirs du scandale" où les dames se reposaient des fatigues de cette vie sociale animée en échangeant des commérages.

Les Assembly Rooms abritent également le Doris Langley Moore's Museum of Costume réputé dans le monde entier, où l'on peut admirer la mode de quatre siècles (photo de gauche).

Tandis que le beau monde dansait et dînait dans les "Assembly Rooms", les riches commerçants de Bath, qui en étaient exclus, se réunissaient dans *le Banqueting Room* (Salle de Banquets) (13) du "Guildhall". Cette salle magnifique de style Adam renferme des portraits de Reynolds et des chandeliers en verre de Whitefriars (photo page 25). Il fut ouvert au public en 1776.

◆ *Pulteney Bridge* (14) (photo page 26) was built by Robert Adam in 1771 following a competition by architects. It is the only bridge in England with shops on both sides and also features three arches and a central Venetian window.

Great Pulteney Street (15) (photo page 27) has been the address of a long line of the famous and infamous. Louis Napoleon, later Napoleon III lived there, so did Mrs Maria Fitzherbert who was secretly married to the Prince of Wales, later King George IV. Other celebrated residents have included Lady Hamilton, Lord Nelson's mistress; William Wilberforce who abolished slavery; and Thomas Baldwin, the Bath city architect who designed Great Pulteney Street. The Holburne and Menstrie Museum crowns the street. It houses an important collection of works of art and is a centre for modern crafts.

◆ *Pulteney Bridge* (14) (Foto Seite 26) wurde 1771 von Robert Adam entworfen. Sie ist die einzige Brücke in England mit Läden auf beiden Seiten. Sie überspannt den Fluß auf drei Bögen und hat ein zentrales venezianisches Fenster.

Great Pulteney Street (15) (Foto Seite 27) kann eine lange Liste berühmter und berüchtigter Einwohner aufweisen. Louis Napoleon, später Napoleon III, und auch Maria Fitzherbert, die heimlich mit dem Prinzen von Wales, dem späteren König George IV, verheiratet war, wohnten hier.

Die Krönung der Straße ist das Holburne and Menstrie Museum mit einer wichtigen Sammlung von Kunstgegenständen. Das Museum ist darüber hinaus ein Zentrum für das moderne Kunstgewerbe.

Auf einem Hügel mit Blick über Bath liegt *Prior Park* (16), ein für den Geschäftsmann Ralph Allen im

◆ *Pulteney Bridge* (14) (photo page 26) a été bâti par Robert Adam en 1771. C'est le seul pont d'Angleterre qui possède des magasins de chaque côté de la rue et comprend trois arches et une fenêtre vénitienne centrale.

De nombreuses personnes, aussi bien célèbres que de mauvaise réputation, ont habité dans *Great Pulteney Street* (15) (photo page 27), dont Louis Napoléon, puis Napoléon III ainsi que Maria Fitzherbert, secrètement mariée au Prince de Galles, qui devint par la suite le roi George IV.

Le Holburne and Menstrie Museum, qui se dresse au bout de cette rue, renferme une collection importante de chefs-d'oeuvre et d'objets d'art moderne.

Sur une colline lointaine dominant Bath se trouve *Prior Park* (16), un château de style palladien construit pour l'homme d'affaires, Ralph Allen.

◆ High on a hill overlooking Bath is *Prior Park* (16), a Palladian style mansion built for the entrepreneur Ralph Allen. After making his fortune in Bath by reforming the British postal system, Allen bought the quarries on Combe Down where the golden stone - oolitic limestone - was mined to build Georgian Bath.

◆ Stil der Palladium-Architektur erbautes Herrenhaus.

Allen kaufte die Steinbrüche am Combe Down, wo der goldene Stein - oolithischer Kalkstein - zum Bau des georgianischen Bath abgebaut wurde.

◆ Allen acheta les carrières de Combe Down, dont les pierres dorées - calcaire oolithique - ont été utilisées pour construire la ville Georgienne de Bath.

Echoes of The Past

◆ Mementoes of the past form a carefully preserved part of Bath's heritage. A mix of humble and high-born people who lived in the city have left an indelible mark on Bath today.

North Parade (17) was the home of Wordsworth the poet, Oliver Goldsmith the novelist and Edmund Burke the statesman.

Favourite areas where fashionable people paraded in their finery included North Parade and also *Gravel Walk* (18) near to the *Royal Victoria Park* (19).

In *Queen's Parade Place* (20) can be seen two stylish pavilions built for waiting sedan chair men to keep them away from the inns and liquor that made them rude and abusive to customers. This attempt at regulation was a forerunner of Hackney Carriage licensing.

The quality shops that line *Milsom Street* (21) built in 1762, made it a fashionable place to shop in the 18th century, just as now.

The National Centre of Photography in Milsom Street was a circulating library and reading rooms where probably Jane Austen enjoyed reading the 'gothic' novels that inspired her Bath-based pastiches.

Broad Street is the home of

Spuren Der Vergangenheit

◆ Andenken an die Vergangenheit bilden einen sorgfältig erhaltenen Teil des Erbes der Stadt Bath. Die Mischung aus einfachen und vornehmen Menschen, die in dieser Stadt wohnten, prägt auch das heutige Bath noch.

North Parade (17) war die Heimat des Poeten Wordsworth, des Romanciers Oliver Goldsmith und des Staatsmanns Edmund Burke.

Auf der North Parade und auch der *Gravel Walk* (18) in der Nähe des *Royal Victoria Park* (19) (Foto Seite 00) trugen modebewußte Mitglieder der Gesellschaft gerne ihre neuesten Kreationen zur Schau.

Auf dem *Queen's Parade Place* (20) befinden sich zwei elegante Pavillons. Sie wurden als Aufenthalt für wartende Sänftenträger gebaut, um diese von den Gasthäusern und dem Alkohol fernzuhalten, der sie ihren Kunden gegenüber rüde und unverschämt werden ließ.

Aufgrund ihrer guten Geschäfte war *Milsom Street* (21) im 18. Jahrhundert eine beliebte Einkaufsstraße, sie ist dies auch heute noch. Das National Centre of Photography in Milsom Street war eine Fahrbücherei und Leseräume. Hier las Jane Austen vielleicht die "gothischen" Romane, die ihre in Bath spielenden Persiflagen inspirierten.

Temoignages du passe

◆ Les témoignages du passé représentent une partie soigneusement préservée du patrimoine de Bath. Un mélange de personnes humbles et riches qui ont vécu dans cette ville ont laissé une marque indélébile encore visible aujourd'hui.

North Parade (17) fut le quartier choisi par le poète Wordsworth, l'auteur Oliver Goldsmith et l'homme d'état Edmund Burke.

"North Parade et *Gravel Walk* (18) à proximité de *Royal Victoria Park* (19) étaient les endroits de prédilection du beau monde pour y faire parade de ses richesses.

A *Queen's Parade Place* (20), on peut voir deux pavillons construits pour les porteurs de chaises à porteurs qui attendaient là pour empêcher qu'ils s'enivrent dans les taveres et insultent les clients.

Les magasins d'articles de qualité de *Milsom Street* (21) firent de cette rue la rue la plus prisée pour les emplettes au 18ème siècle, tout comme aujourd'hui. Le "National Centre of Photography" comprenait une bibliothèque et des salles de lecture où Jane Austen lut probablement avec plaisir les romans "gothiques" qui inspirèrent ses pastiches sur Bath.

Broad Street abrite le *Bath Postal Museum* (22) (photo page 28) où le premier timbre-poste fut utilisé le 2 mai 1840.

East Gate (23), près du fleuve Avon, rappelle les racines médiévales de Bath, C'est à cet endroit de la rivière que les moines qui établirent le commerce prospère des étoffes de laine apportaient les toisons des moutons des Cotswolds.

◆ *Bath Postal Museum* (22) (Photo top left) where the world's first postage stamp was posted on May 2, 1840.

A reminder of Bath's medieval roots can be found near the timeless River Avon. *East Gate* (23) was used by monks who built up the flourishing woollen cloth trade from Cotswold sheep. They brought the fleeces to the river at this point.

Sally Lunn's House (24) in North Parade Passage is the oldest house in Bath (Photo left), now a refreshment house and museum. Roman remains have been found below the cellar floor indicating food was being prepared on the site 1,700 years ago. A medieval faggot oven, probably used to bake bread to feed workmen building the vast Norman Abbey can be seen. The present timber-framed building dates from 1482, but Sally Lunn did not arrive in Bath until 1680 to bake and hawk her brioche buns. Her shop later became a fashionable coffee house, said to be favoured by 'Beau' Nash and Ralph

◆ Allen. The secret recipe for the buns was rediscovered in a panel above the fireplace in 1937 and the buns are now sold as a delicacy.

The bow-fronted merchant's house (now an insurance office) at the corner of Gay Street and *Old King Street* (25) features a small powder room to the right of the front door (Photo page 28). Through the window can be seen Bristol Delft tiles surrounding the powder bowl, which contained powder for wigs - an essential mark of status for the wealthy residents of Bath two centuries ago.

An illuminated scale model (photo below) of Bath's Georgian heritage is the highlight of the *Building of Bath Museum* (26). Opened in 1992, the musuem has a prestigious address: The Countess of Huntingdon's Chapel, The Vineyards, The Paragon.

Visitors can find out how and why and who built Georgian Bath. The displays present a fascinating glimpse of a city's elegant rebirth in the 18th century.

Bath Industrial Heritage Centre (27), (photo page 29) Morford Street in Lansdown, recreates an engineering works at the turn of the century and tells the story of Bath stone.

The theatre (photo above) in Orchard Street (28) was granted the status of a Theatre Royal in 1767. John Palmer, a wealthy brewer and chandler, promoted the idea of a theatre to add to Bath's many attractions.

Bath cultivates its reputation today as a premier heritage centre. Its sublime stone architecture is further enhanced by abundant floral displays and green parkland. *The Botanical Gardens* (29) features an extensive collection of plants from all parts of the world.

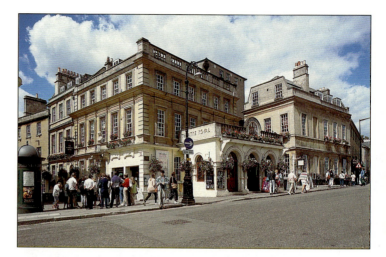

◆ Broad Street ist die Heimat des *Bath Postal Museum* (22) (Foto Seite 28), wo am 2. Mai 1840 die erste Briefmarke der Welt aufgegeben wurde.

East Gate (23) in der Nähe des zeitlosen Avons erinnert an die mittelalterliche Verwurzelung von Bath. Sie wurde von Mönchen benutzt, die den blühenden Wolltuchhandel mit Wolle von Schafen aus den Cotswolds aufbauten und an dieser Stelle die Vliese zum Fluß brachten.

Das Haus der Sally Lunn (24) (Foto Seite 29) in der North Parade Passage ist das älteste Haus in Bath, es dient heute als "Erfrischungshaus" und Museum. Unter dem Kellerboden wurden Überreste aus römischer Zeit gefunden, die darauf schließen lassen, daß an dieser Stelle schon vor 1.700 Jahren Lebensmittel zubereitet wurden. Ein mittelalterlicher Ofen ist zu sehen, der mit Reisigbündeln geheizt wurde. Er diente eventuell zum Backen von Brot für die Arbeiter beim Bau der riesigen normannischen Abtei. Das heutige Fachwerkgebäude stammt aus dem Jahr 1482. Sally Lunn kam aber erst 1680 nach Bath, um ihre berühmten "Buns" (Brioches) zu backen und zu verkaufen. Ihr Laden wurde später zu einem modischen Café, das angeblich häufig von "Beau" Nash und Ralph Allen besucht wurde. Das Geheimrezept für die Brioches wurde 1937 in einem Paneel über dem Kamin wiederentdeckt. Heute werden die "Buns" als Delikatesse verkauft.

Im Kaufmannshaus mit dem Erker (heute ein Versicherungsbüro) an der Ecke von Gay Street und *Old King Street* (25) befindet sich rechts von der Eingangstür ein kleines Puderzimmer (Foto Seite 28). Durch das Fenster kann man eine von Delfter Kacheln umgebene Puderschale sehen, in der Puder für Perücken - vor zwei Jahrhunderten ein unerläßliches Statuskennzeichen für die reichen Einwohner von Bath - aufbewahrt wurde.

Ein beleuchtetes maßstabgetreues Modell (Foto links) des georgianischen Erbes der Stadt ist das Prachtstück im *Building of Bath Museum* (26). Hier können Besucher herausfinden, wie, warum und wer die Gebäude des georgianischen Bath baute. Die Ausstellungsstücke stellen einen faszinierenden Einblick in die Neugeburt einer eleganten Stadt im 18. Jahrhundert dar.

Im *Bath Industrial Heritage Centre*, (Foto Seite 29) Morford Street in Lansdown (27), sind Bauarbeiten aus der Zeit der Jahrhundertwende ausgestellt. Hier wird die Geschichte des Bath-Steins erzählt.

Das Theater (Foto oben) in der Orchard Street (28) wurde 1767 zu einem Theatre Royal, einem königlichen Theater, erhoben. John Palmer, ein reicher Brauereibesitzer und Schiffsausrüster, förderte die Idee eines Theaters, um die vielen Attraktionen von Bath noch zu vermehren.

Bath kultiviert heute seine Reputation als ein führendes historisches Zentrum. Seine unübertroffene Steinarchitektur wird durch eine Fülle von Blumen- und Grünanlagen noch verschönert. *Die Botanical Gardens* (Botanischen Gärten) (29) enthalten eine umfassende Sammlung von Pflanzen aus allen Teilen der Welt.

◆ *La maison de Sally Lunn* (24) (photo page 29), dans "North Parade Passage", qui est la plus ancienne de Bath, est maintenant un salon de thé et un musée. Des vestiges romains retrouvés sous le plancher de la cave indiquent que l'on cuisinait déjà à cet endroit il y a 1700 ans. On peut y voir un four à bois médiéval, probablement utilisé pour faire le pain pour les ouvriers construisant la vaste Abbaye romane. L'édifice actuel dont la charpente est en bois remonte à 1482, mais Sally Lunn n'arriva à Bath qu'en 1680 pour faire ses brioches et les colporter. Son magasin devint par la suite un salon de thé à la mode, fréquenté par "Beau" Nash et Ralph Allen. La recette secrète de ses brioches fut redécouverte dans un panneau au-dessus de la cheminée en 1937 et on peut à nouveau apprécier ces délicieuses gourmandises.

La maison marchande à façade en saillie (actuellement un bureau d'assurances) à l'angle de Gay Street et *d'Old King Street* (25) possède des toilettes de petite taille à droite de la porte d'entrée (Photo page 28). On peut y voir, par la fenêtre, la cuvette qui contenait la poudre pour perruques, entourée de carreaux en faïence de Delft - symbole de prestige important pour les riches résidents de Bath il y a 200 ans.

La maquette illuminée du patrimoine de la ville Georgienne de Bath (photo page 30) est le clou du *Building of Bath Museum* (26).

Les visiteurs peuvent ainsi découvrir qui construisit la ville Georgienne de Bath, et pourquoi et comment elle fut construite. Cette maquette donne un aperçu fascinant du renouveau de cette ville au 18ème siècle, qui lui donna son caractère raffiné.

Le Bath Industrial Heritage Centre (photo page 29) dans Morford Street à Lansdown (27) recrée une usine du fin 19ème-début 20ème siècle et raconte l'histoire de la pierre de Bath.

Le théâtre (photo page 30) dans Orchard Street (28) a reçu le statut de Théâtre Royal en 1767. John Palmer, brasseur et marchand de fournitures pour bateaux, promut l'idée d'un théâtre pour compléter les nombreux divertissements offerts par Bath.

Bath cultive aujourd'hui sa réputation de centre historique par excellence. Son architecture sublime en pierre est rehaussée par ses massifs de fleurs et ses parcs. *Les "Botanical Gardens"* (29) comprennent une vaste sélection de plantes des quatre coins du monde.

Beyond Bath

◆ Three miles from the city is the American Museum at Claverton Manor. It recreates domestic life in America from the late 17th to 19th centuries and the work of American craftsmen (Photo below).

This classical building, designed by Sir Jeffry Wyatville, was built in 1820.

Beckford's Tower, built in 1827 on Lansdown Hill, gives extensive views over the city.

Within an hour's drive from Bath are the cities of Bristol and Wells; Cheddar Gorge and stately homes including Dyrham Park, Corsham Court and Longleat; Stourhead Gardens; the villages of Castle Combe and Lacock and the ancient monuments of Stonehenge and Avebury.

Bath - Seine Umgebung

◆ In Claverton Manor, ca. 5 km außerhalb der Stadt, befindet sich das American Museum. Hier werden Haushaltsgegenstände und Wohnungseinrichtungen gezeigt, die das häusliche Leben in Amerika in der Zeit vom Ende des 17. Jahrhunderts bis zum 19. Jahrhundert wiedergeben, sowie die Arbeiten amerikanischer Handwerker (Foto oben).

Dieses klassische Gebäude wurde von Sir Jeffry Wyatville entworfen und 1820 erbaut.

Beckford's Tower wurde 1827 auf Lansdown Hill erbaut und bietet einen weiten Blick über die Stadt.

Im Umkreis von einer Autostunde von Bath liegen die Städte Bristol und Wells, Cheddar Gorge (Höhlen) und verschiedene Herrenhäuser, darunter Dyrham Park, Corsham Court und Longleat, Stourhead Gardens, die Ortschaften Castle Combe und Lacock und die historischen Denkmäler Stonehenge und Avebury.

Périphérie de Bath

◆ A cinq kilomètres de cette ville se trouve l'American Museum à Claverton Manor. Il recrée la vie domestique en Amérique de la fin du 17ème au 19ème siècle et présente le travail d'artisans américains (Photo ci-dessus.

Cet édifice classique, conçu par sir Jeffry Wyatville, a été construit en 1820.

Beckford's Tower, construit en 1827, sur la colline de Lansdown, offre une vue magnifique sur la ville.

A une heure de voiture de Bath, se trouvent Bristol et Wells; "Cheddar Gorge" et les châteaux de "Dyrham Park", "Corsham Court" et "Longleat"; "Stourhead Gardens"; les villages de Castle Combe et Lacock et les anciens monuments de Stonehenge et Avebury.